Dams and Hydropower

Development or DESTRUCTION?

Dams and Hydropower

Louise Spilsbury

rosen publishing's
rosen central

NEW YORK

This edition first published in 2012 by:

The Rosen Publishing Group, Inc.
29 East 21st Street, New York, NY 10010

**Library of Congress
Cataloging-in-Publication Data**

Spilsbury, Louise,
Dams and hydropower/Louise Spilsbury.—1st ed.
    p. cm.—(Development or destruction?)
Includes bibliographical references and index.
ISBN 978-1-4488-6990-9 (library binding)—
ISBN 978-1-4488-6994-7 (pbk.)—
ISBN 978-1-4488-6995-4 (6-pack)
1. Dams—Juvenile literature. 2. Water-power—Juvenile literature. I. Spilsbury, Louise. II. Title.
TC540.S65 2012
627'.8—dc23

2011037052

Manufactured in the United States of America

CPSIA Compliance Information: Batch #W12YA: For further information, contact Rosen Publishing, New York, New York, at 1-800-237-9932.

Picture acknowledgments:

The author and publisher would like to thank the following agencies for allowing these pictures to be reproduced: Alamy/Images of Africa Photobank: p22; Alamy/Vicent Pellicer Ollés: p36; Alamy/Global Warming Images: p41; Alamy/Prixpics: p42; Alamy/An Qi: p43; Corbis/Galen Rowell: p13; Corbis/Stringer Shanghai/Reuters: p30; Corbis/Suthep Kritsanavarin/epa: p40; Getty/Nikki Kahn/The Washington Post: p5, pp21–21/5; Getty/Brent Stirton: p14; Getty/AFP: p19; Getty/Frederic J. Brown/AFP: 31; Getty/Jaime Reina/AFP: p37; iStock: pp10–11, p28, p35, p38; Shutterstock: front cover, p3, p4, p6, pp6–7, p8, p9, p12, p16, p18, p22, p23, p25, pp26–27, p32, p34, p36, p39, p41. All locator maps: Shutterstock.

Images used throughout for creative graphics: iStockphoto, Shutterstock.
Should there be any inadvertent omission, please apply to the publisher for rectification.

Contents

Water and dams

Water is the most important natural resource on Earth. Fresh water is essential to human life, for drinking, sanitation, industry and irrigation, and also for generating electricity. Everyone needs water, but water is not evenly distributed in rivers or underground sources around the world.

Rain doesn't fall evenly globally, within the same country, or throughout the year. So for thousands of years people have been looking for ways to extract, control or increase the supplies of fresh water. One of the ways they do this is by building dams.

▲ Water is a vital resource for growing food and other crops, as in this heavily irrigated cotton field in Arizona.

Dams at work

Dams are structures that are built across rivers, estuaries or streams to retain water. Dams vary from small earth embankments, often built for farm use, to large concrete structures. Water trapped behind a dam is stored in a reservoir. Water from the reservoir can then be piped to homes, factories or farms, or used for hydropower. Dams control water flow to prevent flooding after heavy storms and increase the water depth of a river so that ships and barges can travel along it more easily. Reservoirs are used as sites for sports such as swimming, boating and fishing. Many dams are multipurpose, which means they provide two or more of the above benefits.

Chapter 1

Big dams

One of the world's oldest known dams was the Jawa Dam, built from rock and earth in Jordan in 4 BCE. It held back water from a small stream so that local farmers could use it for irrigation. Small dams like this are still built, but during the twentieth century people began to build dams on a much larger scale. In fact, apart from he Great Wall of China, dams are the biggest structures people have ever made. A large dam is one that is higher than 16 yards (15 meters), which is as tall as, or taller than, a four-story building, and there are over 40,000 large dams worldwide. There are also more than 300 mega-dams globally – these are the giants of the dam world, each with a minimum height of 164 yards (150 meters)!

Development fact

Worldwide, 30 to 40 percent of irrigated land relies on dams, which means that around 800 million people eat food produced using water obtained from dams.

▽ **The Cap-de-Long Dam, the biggest dam in the Pyrenees Mountains, France.**

Dams worldwide

There are several reasons why there was a boom in big dam building in the twentieth century. One was technological – it became easier to make giant, strong dams using poured, reinforced cement rather than bricks and mortar. Another was population growth and the need for more land for farming and settlements. Damming big rivers could prevent flooding, provide irrigation and enable larger ships to navigate upriver. A major reason for dam building is for supplying hydropower, because providing a country with electricity supports industrial and economic growth. In addition, many poor countries can afford to build dams to develop their economies using loans from organizations such as the World Bank.

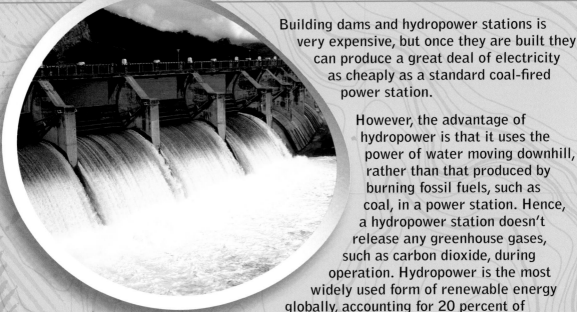

Building dams and hydropower stations is very expensive, but once they are built they can produce a great deal of electricity as cheaply as a standard coal-fired power station.

However, the advantage of hydropower is that it uses the power of water moving downhill, rather than that produced by burning fossil fuels, such as coal, in a power station. Hence, a hydropower station doesn't release any greenhouse gases, such as carbon dioxide, during operation. Hydropower is the most widely used form of renewable energy globally, accounting for 20 percent of world electricity overall.

▲ Hydropower converts the energy of moving water into electricity.

Countries with hills and large, fast-flowing rivers such as Canada and Norway generate over 80 percent of their electricity using hydropower. In remote mountainous communities, such as in Himalayan villages, hydropower is often the only source of electricity.

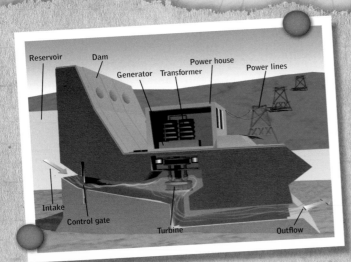

Reservoir Dam Generator Transformer Power house Power lines Intake Control gate Turbine Outflow

How hydropower works

Hydroelectric power stations, which generate hydroelectric power, are built next to dams. Inside the dam, valves open and release some of the water from the reservoir through tunnels in the dam. Because of the weight of the deep water in the reservoir and the drop in height from the high dam down through the tunnels, the moving water is under high pressure. This pushing power turns turbines – similar to propellers – which rotate machines called generators. These convert the spinning energy into electricity.

Destruction fact

It is estimated that 40 to 80 million people have been displaced by dams. At present up to 2 million people are displaced every year by large dams.

▽ Dams bring benefits and problems all over the world. The five case studies in this book look at some of the major issues and impacts associated with dams today.

Pros and cons of dams

The pace of dam building globally has slowed down since the 1990s because people began to doubt that the development benefits they bring outweigh the human and environmental destruction they cause. For example, huge numbers of people are displaced from their land to make way for reservoirs, or they lose their livelihoods when water and therefore fish stocks are reduced downstream of a dam.

We're going to explore whether destruction is always an inevitable consequence of development or whether people can build dams to sustain our societies without degrading the natural environment. Is a new dam development or destruction?

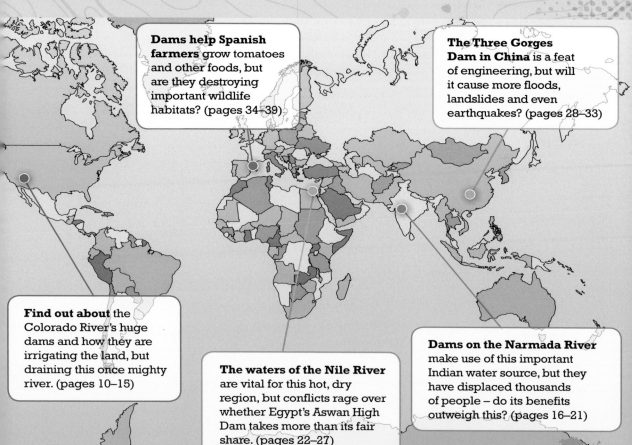

Dams help Spanish farmers grow tomatoes and other foods, but are they destroying important wildlife habitats? (pages 34–39)

The Three Gorges Dam in China is a feat of engineering, but will it cause more floods, landslides and even earthquakes? (pages 28–33)

Find out about the Colorado River's huge dams and how they are irrigating the land, but draining this once mighty river. (pages 10–15)

The waters of the Nile River are vital for this hot, dry region, but conflicts rage over whether Egypt's Aswan High Dam takes more than its fair share. (pages 22–27)

Dams on the Narmada River make use of this important Indian water source, but they have displaced thousands of people – do its benefits outweigh this? (pages 16–21)

Colorado River dams, US

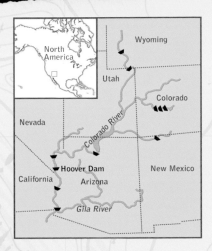

This map shows the location of the Colorado River and the dams along its length.

The Colorado River is one of the longest rivers in the US. It springs from the Rocky Mountains in the north and runs 1,450 miles (2,330 km) through seven western states into the Gulf of California in Mexico. The river is a vital source of water because most of the regions that it runs through receive little annual rainfall.

Dam building

A series of 20 dams was built on the Colorado River and its tributaries during the twentieth century. Water in the Colorado basin comes from snow on the mountain ranges, and dams stopped the flooding of the river and its tributaries that could occur in spring when the snow melted. The dams also ensured there was more water available for the dry summer months, and hydropower from the dams supplied electricity to the growing population in the region.

The largest, the Hoover Dam, was completed in 1936 and was the first multipurpose mega-dam to be built. Thousands came to construct it and a new city, Boulder City, grew up to house these workers. The second largest dam, Glen Canyon Dam, began operating in 1964.

Chapter 2

Development fact

Around 25 percent of US food is grown on land irrigated by water from the Colorado River.

Between them, these two dams store about four-fifths of the water held in reservoirs in the Colorado River Basin.

Diversions and development

The dams built along the Colorado River transformed the region. They helped turn dry deserts, such as Arizona and Nevada, into places where people could live and farm, and they provided the water and power necessary for economic development. Pipes and aqueducts transport water far from the river and have allowed populations to expand in cities such as Denver, Los Angeles and Phoenix. The water is used for drinking, cooking and sanitation systems and also to fill swimming pools and water gardens. The cheap hydropower provided by the dams was vital for the expansion of manufacturing industries in Arizona, such as mining, communications and electronics.

Dams can also be good for tourism development. Over a million tourists a year visit the Hoover Dam itself, and more come to its reservoir, Lake Mead, for recreational activities like swimming, fishing and boating.

Canals divert water from the river to huge agricultural areas in Nevada, California and Arizona. The All-American Canal is the largest irrigation canal in the world. It runs 80 miles (129 km) from the river into the Imperial Valley, California. The valley was once a wasteland, but its 3,000 miles (5,000 km) of irrigation canals have turned it into rich farmland that generates more than a billion dollars in farm income each year.

Colorado water flow decreases

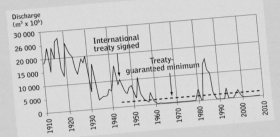

Discharge (m³ x 10⁶)

The graph above shows the amount of water from the Colorado River flowing into Mexico between 1910 and 2010. In 1944 a treaty guaranteed at least 1.85 billion cubic m (1.5 million acre feet) of water for Mexico each year (this minimum amount is shown by a dotted line on the graph). As you can see from the graph's continuous line, water flow has dropped since the 1920s (apart from a temporary increase in the 1980s, thought to be due to wet weather and an efficiency drive). The drop in water flow was caused by agricultural and industrial demands in the southwestern US and the fact that the area's population tripled, as shown by the graph below.

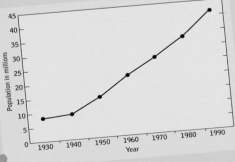

An overtapped resource

The dams along the Colorado River helped develop the region, but they have caused problems, too. The river water is drying up, partly because consumption is increasing as a result of growing populations and changing water demands, for example, for new golf courses. And, because the US government has subsidized water for farmers and ranchers, many have used irrigation water inefficiently, growing thirsty crops unsuitable for arid regions, such as rice, cotton and alfalfa.

Water flow in the river is also reduced because large amounts of water evaporate from the surface of Colorado reservoirs due to the dry desert climate. Around 20 percent of the river's annual flow is lost to evaporation and seepage from its reservoir system.

The Mexican delta region

Around 90 percent of the Colorado River's water is extracted before it even reaches the Mexican border, and most years the river no longer reaches the sea. This has had a major impact on the river's delta region in northern Mexico. Deltas form when rivers slow where they meet the sea and sediment is deposited on land. Without sufficient deposition, the sea gradually washes the delta away into the sea. Water extraction upriver of the Colorado is drying out the delta.

This image of the Colorado River and its tributaries shows the generally arid setting of the delta region at the Sea of Cortez, Baja, Mexico.

The loss of the delta and reduction in river flow have had a major impact on northern Mexico. Native American tribes, such as the Cucapa, lived off fishing. Today, abandoned fishing boats litter the dried-up delta, and the loss of water has robbed tens of thousands of local fishermen of their livelihoods. Now agriculture is the main industry in the Mexicali valley that straddles the vast Colorado River Delta, but the reduction in water supply means that Mexican farmers are suffering from drought. Also, the water supply for rapidly growing cities like Mexicali, Tijuana, Tecate and Rosarito has been compromised.

ON THE SCENE

"When the river disappeared, so did our lives and culture."

Inocencia Gonzalez, Cucapa village chief, 2011

Destruction fact

The Colorado River Delta was once home to abundant plant and animal life, but now just 5 percent of its original area remains.

Dams and Hydropower

Managing the Colorado River

The situation for the Colorado River is likely to worsen, in part due to climate change, which is set to increase the amount of surface water lost by evaporation. Scientists from the University of Washington predict the flow of the Colorado River will decline by one-third by 2050. The region has to find ways to ensure there is enough water in the river for the US and Mexico to use and has to work at improving the water quality.

Water savings

Governments are trying different ways to save water, for example, storing water in underground aquifers to minimize loss of water by evaporation from surface reservoirs. Water authorities have paid businesses, such as golf clubs, to remove grass from golf courses. Higher prices encourage people to use less water, too. Water bills for farmers in San Diego rose by 40 percent within two years. The increased revenue helped the local water authority pay for new concrete-lined sections of the All-American Canal to reduce seepage.

The Coachella Main Canal, which carries water from the All-American Canal to the Coachella Valley in California.

EXPLORE FURTHER

Find out about the Bakun hydropower dam, which is generating jobs but reducing water flow in the Rajang River in Borneo.

Water agreements

One barrier to progress is conflicting interests. For example, industries feel it is unfair that farmers in southern California own over 75 percent of the water from the river (due to agreements drawn up in 1922 that gave farmers priority), and farmers in the US don't want more water to go to Mexico. In 2011, Mexican and US governments started to work out a new agreement about managing the river and improving the river's flow, but some people are calling for the removal of the dams altogether.

Development or Destruction?

Development:

* Colorado dams have helped to reduce flooding and store water for the dry summer months.
* A quarter of US food is grown on land irrigated by Colorado River water.
* Hydropower has allowed populations to grow and industries to flourish.
* Colorado dams allow people to live and farm in US desert regions.
* The dams bring economic development through tourism.

Destruction:

* The Colorado River is drying up because the dams allow ever-increasing water withdrawals.
* Reservoirs waste water by evaporation and seepage.
* When water has been subsidized, farmers grow thirsty crops.
* The US takes so much water that the river runs dry in Mexico and the Colorado River Delta, so wetland habitats are drying up.
* The lack of river water is negatively impacting Mexican farmers, fishermen and cities.

Monsoon rains

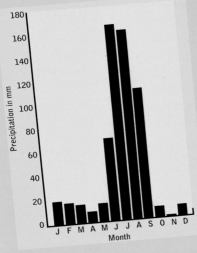

This graph shows the average monthly precipitation levels for New Delhi, the capital of India. In India most rain falls in one short season called the monsoon. The monsoon usually begins in June, brings heavy downpours in July and August, and tails off from September. Supporters of dams say that reservoirs are the only large-scale method of storing monsoon water for year-round use.

The construction of large dams on the Narmada River in central India has had a major impact on millions of people living in the river valley. The question of whether these dams are a force for development or destruction has become the focus of furious debate in India and worldwide.

Water in India

There is a lot of pressure on the Indian government to provide water to improve the lives of its people. At present, one-fifth of the population doesn't have safe drinking water and two-thirds of the population lack basic sanitation.

The Narmada River runs through three Indian states – Madhya Pradesh, Maharashtra and Gujarat – before flowing into the Indian Ocean. Many of these areas are prone to drought; for example, parts of Gujarat often use tankers to bring drinking water to its people. Governments began to build dams along the Narmada and its 41 tributaries in the 1980s.

A woman from Gujarat washing clothes in a reservoir.

Chapter 3

Development fact

The hydropower stations at Sardar Sarovar dam were designed to provide a maximum electricity output of 1,450 megawatts. This would be enough power to supply up to 1.3 million US homes with electricity for a year. An average person in India uses around 1/25th of the power an average American uses, so in theory the dam could provide power for tens of millions of Indians.

Narmada Valley development plan

The dam-building project planned to build over 3,000 small, medium and large dams by 2025, the biggest of which is the Sardar Sarovar Dam. The project also included the construction of the largest canal in the world, the Narmada Main Canal, running 280 miles (450 km) from the Sardar Sarovar Dam to Gujarat.

Supporters say the benefits of the Narmada Valley dam project are obvious. They say it will provide drinking water for the 18 million people living in the area today and even for the 40 million who could be living there, as the population increases, by 2020. It will irrigate 4.5–4.7 million acres (1.8–1.9 million ha) of land – an area the size of the southeast of England – and thus feed about 20 million people. Hydropower from the dams will provide electricity to regions that used to receive only erratic and limited supplies, if any at all, and help Indian industries to develop and create jobs for India's millions of unemployed.

Vital statistics:

Sardar Sarovar Dam

Height: 133 yards (122 m)
Reservoir length: 133 miles (214 km)
Land submerged: 357,685 acres (144,750 ha)
Forest submerged: 139,615 acres (56,500 ha)
Cost: Over $4 billion of the Gujarat government's irrigation budget

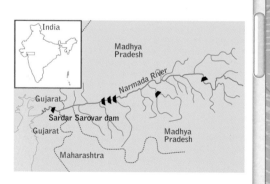

Dams and Hydropower

Displacement and destruction

Critics of the dams, and the Sardar Sarovar Dam in particular, say any benefits came at a high cost. They opposed the project mainly because building the dams and reservoirs would displace farmers from land. The project would also have many other impacts, such as submerging forests where rare wildlife, such as tigers, live and increasing areas of standing water where disease-carrying insects could breed.

To build the Sardar Sarovar Dam and reservoir meant large areas of land had to be flooded, some of which was productive agricultural land or land that had historic or cultural significance to the communities who lived there. Around 320,000 poor rural landowners were paid to leave. Their compensation was often simply the value of lost crops, or they were given lower-quality farmland elsewhere. Communities were broken up as families moved to new places to live and work. If people didn't own the land they lived or worked on, or if it wasn't immediately within the dam zone, they got no compensation. For example, people lost their land without compensation when new roads or storage areas for goods, such as the cement for the dam, were built on it.

▽ **When forests and land were flooded to create the Sardar Sarovar Dam and reservoir, people and wild animals, such as already endangered Indian tigers, lost their homes and livelihoods.**

Protest and progress

Protest against the project was led by the Narmada Bachhao Andolan, or NBA (Save the Narmada Movement), which organized marches, sit-ins and fasts. There was even a documentary film made, called *Drowned Out* (2002), which followed one tribal family who stayed to face drowning rather than make way for the dam. Some protestors were attacked with sticks and tear gas by police and imprisoned. Other organizations, such as the Environmental Defense Fund (EDF), fought the dam on the grounds that important biodiversity would be lost if the Narmada Valley was flooded.

NBA protesters outside the United Nations (UN) building in New Delhi in 2000. One of the NBA's slogans was "*Vikas chahiye, vinash nahin*," which means "We want development, not destruction."

After an international outcry, the World Bank withdrew funding from the project in 1993, and the Indian Supreme Court stopped construction in 1995, only to allow it to go ahead again in 1999. After this, protestors focused on rehabilitating displaced people and keeping the height of the Sardar Sarovar Dam down, because every time the dam was built higher, more land was inundated with water and more people were displaced. The NBA has fought height increases in court several times, and in 2011 was still fighting the building of extra gates on top of the dam that will increase its height further. They also support displaced people who are fighting for compensation.

Destruction fact

Around 1 million people from 245 villages were threatened with displacement by the Narmada dams project.

Dams and Hydropower

Environmental compensation

To compensate for the forest land submerged by the proposed reservoir, the Indian government enlarged the Shoolpaneshwar Wildlife Sanctuary four times and planted trees on large areas of unforested land in the sanctuary. This should benefit wildlife, such as rare sloth bears, in the region. However, some say it has created additional problems for local people, even though the government also plans to provide mobile clinics and schools. Under Indian wildlife laws, people living on sanctuary lands are no longer allowed to collect wood, which is vital for cooking and heating homes, nor can they repair roads and bridges. In practice, many will no longer be able to live in the area.

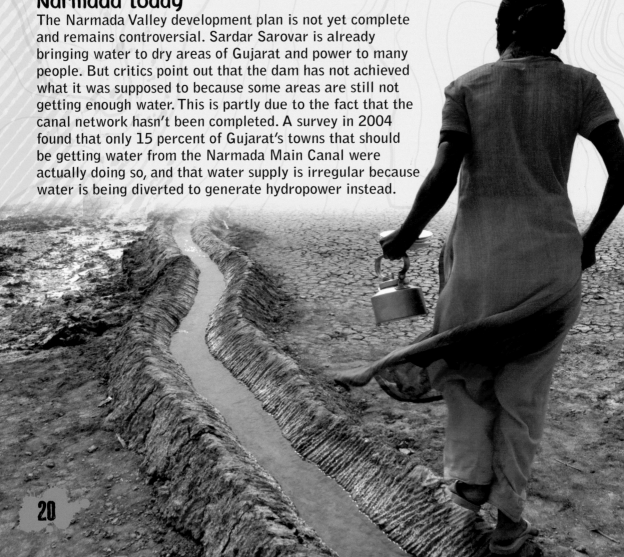

Critics say that so far the Sardar Sarovar Dam has not fulfilled its promise of bringing plentiful water to dry areas such as the Kutch region in Gujarat.

Narmada today

The Narmada Valley development plan is not yet complete and remains controversial. Sardar Sarovar is already bringing water to dry areas of Gujarat and power to many people. But critics point out that the dam has not achieved what it was supposed to because some areas are still not getting enough water. This is partly due to the fact that the canal network hasn't been completed. A survey in 2004 found that only 15 percent of Gujarat's towns that should be getting water from the Narmada Main Canal were actually doing so, and that water supply is irregular because water is being diverted to generate hydropower instead.

Narmada Valley dams, India

EXPLORE FURTHER

Find out about the Polavaram dam and Godavari River in Andhra Pradesh, India. This project will affect 7,400 acres (3,000 ha) of forest and around 250 villages if it goes ahead.

Who benefits?

Critics say local water projects, which cause minimal environmental damage, are just as effective as building dams and are less destructive. One alternative is for farmers to use rainwater harvesting (collecting) schemes to irrigate crops. Furthermore, in October 2010 Medha Patkar, leader of the NBA, said there were 40,000 families that had lived in the submergence area and were waiting to be resettled. So the question is, do the benefits of the Narmada dams outweigh the costs of displacement of people and loss of wildlife?

Development or Destruction?

Development:

* Dams are one way to solve India's urgent water problem.
* Narmada dams could provide drinking water for 18 million people, irrigate millions of acres (hectares) of land and feed millions of people.
* Hydropower from Sardar Sarovar Dam could bring electricity to industries and to homes that have never previously had any.
* The expanded Shoolpaneshwar Wildlife Sanctuary goes toward compensating for lost wildlife habitat.

Destruction:

* Dams are expensive - Sardar Sarovar Dam cost over $4 billion to build.
* The dams do not yet provide the water and power people were told they would.
* Up to 1 million people have been displaced by the project. Many say compensation was inadequate, and others were neither compensated nor resettled.
* The expansion of the Shoolpaneshwar Wildlife Sanctuary meant many tribal people were displaced.

Aswan High Dam, Egypt

The Aswan High Dam is built on the Nile River, the river that supplies 90 percent of Egypt's fresh water and is responsible for the country's development from its earliest times.

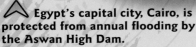

In the past, the river flooded the Nile Valley once a year, depositing an estimated 44 million tons (40 million tonnes) of sediment on the land. This created fertile soil that ancient Egyptians used to grow wheat and other crops. People in the settlements that developed on the Nile also used the river for transport. The Nile is still vital to Egypt today – it provides one-third of its economy, and farming here is completely reliant on irrigation and the river.

Egypt's capital city, Cairo, is protected from annual flooding by the Aswan High Dam.

Vital statistics:

Aswan High Dam

Cost: $1 billion
Length: 12,570 ft (3,830 m)
Height: 364 ft (111 m – higher than a 30-story building)
Reservoir capacity: 90,000,000 acre ft (111 cubic km)

Chapter 4

Aswan High Dam

Aswan, the biggest, most famous dam in Egypt, took 10 years to build; it opened in 1971. To create its reservoir, Lake Nasser, a valley over 342 miles (550 km) long in Egypt and Sudan was flooded – that's about the direct distance between London and Edinburgh. Around 90,000 Egyptian farmers and Sudanese nomads were displaced and relocated, and the huge, ancient Egyptian temple complex of Abu Simbel had to be dismantled and moved.

Development fact

Its positive impact on flooding and food supplies meant that the Aswan High Dam lessened the effects of dangerous floods in 1964 and 1973 and of the threatening droughts in 1972–73 and 1983–84.

Development and the dam

The Aswan High Dam was built to prevent flooding, provide water for people, irrigation for crops and generate electricity. Before it was built, the annual flood waters could destroy entire crops. Given that most of Egypt's population lies along the Nile, the dam has also prevented the river from flooding their homes. The dam collects the flood waters and releases, on average, 44.5 million acre ft (55 billion cubic m) of water per year, of which around 37.3 million acre ft (46 billion cubic m) are diverted into irrigation canals. The increased productivity due to irrigation from the dam meant the high cost of the dam was paid off in a few years.

Water from the Aswan High Dam is carried to fields along irrigation channels like this.

The dam generates enormous amounts of hydropower. When the dam first reached peak output in 1974, it met 50 percent of Egypt's entire electricity needs. It also allowed many rural Egyptian villages to access electricity for the first time. In addition, Lake Nasser reservoir supports fishing and tourism industries.

ON THE SCENE

"The Nile is everything to us; it's liquid gold. We're like fish here: take us from the water and we'll perish."

Omar, Egyptian fruit farmer, 2010

Problems with the dam

The dam has also created a variety of problems. Now that flood waters and the sediment they carry are trapped behind the dam, farmers use 1 million tons of artificial fertilizers in order to keep soil fertile. Most chemical fertilizers are imported and expensive, and runoff pollutes the river and local environment. Without an annual supply of sediment, farmland on riverbanks downstream of the dam is being eroded. The Nile Delta, where the Nile meets the Mediterranean Sea, is reducing in size and fertility.

Water disputes

One of the biggest problems the dam causes is disputes with neighboring countries. The Nile River has two main tributaries: the Blue Nile, which runs from Ethiopia, and the White Nile, which runs from Lake Victoria, Uganda. Altogether, the Nile and its tributaries flow 4,000 miles (6,500 km) through 10 countries: Uganda, Egypt, Sudan, Ethiopia, the Democratic Republic of Congo (DRC), Tanzania, Kenya, Burundi, Rwanda and Eritrea. It's a vital water and energy source for all these countries, and some are fighting for a bigger share of it.

Water treaties

In 1929 Britain, representing its then East African colonies, signed an agreement with Egypt saying that no country should undertake projects that would reduce the amount of water reaching Egypt.

This map shows the countries through which the White Nile, the Blue Nile and the Nile flow.

Aswan High Dam, Egypt

In 1959 Egypt signed another agreement with Sudan giving Egypt 87 percent of the Nile's flow and Sudan the rest. The other Nile basin countries are now independent and say it's unfair that they should conform to an old colonial treaty in which they had no say, especially as some are among the world's poorest regions. In 2008 the per capita income in Egypt was $1,800, while in Ethiopia it was just $280. Although Ethiopia contributes up to 85 percent of the Nile's waters, it has been unable to use the river to boost development.

Egyptians argue that without the water their region would be desert, whereas some upstream countries are green and lush, like Congo with its rainforests. Egypt claims to be making the most of its water through water recycling and desalination programs. Critics say Egypt overuses and wastes water on unnecessary projects, such as luxury residential developments that have water-intensive landscaped gardens and golf courses.

This is Murchison Falls, where the Nile bursts through a narrow gorge in Uganda's Rift Valley. Uganda and other riparian countries of the Nile want to build irrigation and hydropower projects without having to seek Egypt's approval.

Conflict or compromise?

Major river basins

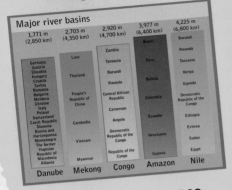

Danube 1,771 m (2,850 km)	Mekong 2,703 m (4,350 km)	Congo 2,920 m (4,700 km)	Amazon 3,977 m (6,400 km)	Nile 4,225 m (6,800 km)
Germany	Laos	Zambia	Brazil	Burundi
Austria	Thailand	Tanzania	Peru	Rwanda
Slovakia		Burundi		Tanzania
Hungary		Rwanda	Bolivia	Kenya
Croatia		Central African Republic		Uganda
Serbia	People's Republic of China		Colombia	
Romania		Cameroon		Democratic Republic of the Congo
Bulgaria				
Moldova			Ecuador	Ethiopia
Ukraine		Angola		
Italy	Cambodia			Eritrea
Poland		Democratic Republic of the Congo	Venezuela	
Switzerland				Sudan
Czech Republic	Vietnam			
Slovenia				
Bosnia and Hertzegovina		Republic of the Congo	Guyana	Egypt
Montenegro				
The former Yugoslav Republic of Macedonia	Myanmar			
Albania				

Globally, there are 263 river basins shared by two or more countries. As you can see from the table, they include many of the world's largest and most important rivers.

Only 105 countries have transboundary agreements in place, without which there can be tensions. However, so far there have only been around 40 cases of reported violence between states over water, and it is hoped that more will cooperate in the future. For example, the countries along the Senegal River – Senegal, Mali, Mauritania and Guinea – share the costs and benefits of jointly operated dams, such as the Manantali Dam in Mali.

Potential conflicts

The Nile Basin Initiative (NBI) is a partnership of the riparian states of the Nile River. It seeks to make agreements on hydropower and irrigation projects on the Nile and to replace the 1929 and 1959 treaties. In 2010, some of the Nile basin countries signed an agreement about using the Nile's resources to improve the livelihoods of all the basin countries' populations. However, Egypt and Sudan have so far refused to sign any agreements, unless they are guaranteed their existing water quota. Egypt says the Nile waters are a matter of national security and that it has the right to take action against countries that dam the river.

EXPLORE FURTHER

Learn more about why China has not joined the Mekong River Commission and why downstream countries complain that Chinese dams reduce their water supplies.

Development or Destruction?

Development:

* The Aswan High Dam prevents the Nile River from flooding.
* The dam provides water for irrigation, which makes it possible to farm in the desert and has lessened the impact of drought years.
* The dam generates enormous amounts of hydropower.
* Lake Nasser supports the fishing and tourism industries.

Destruction:

* Building the dam displaced 90,000 people.
* Without flood water sediment, farmers have to use costly artificial fertilizers. Fertilizer runoff causes pollution.
* Without flood water sediment, riverbanks are eroding, and the Nile Delta is reducing in size and fertility.
* Increases in sea level due to climate change could submerge a fifth of the delta.
* The dam causes disputes with other Nile countries that need water.

Many tourists take boat trips around Lake Nasser to see the archaeological sites along its banks.

Three Gorges Dam, China

The Three Gorges Dam is built across the Yangtze River, the longest river in Asia and the third longest in the world. The Yangtze carries a vast amount of water, and much of it flows through mountains, giving it great potential for hydropower. China built the Three Gorges Dam for flood control, hydropower and to increase the navigability of the Yangtze River.

Flood control

In the past, during monsoon rains, the Yangtze and its tributaries spilled over onto the land and caused terrible floods. In the twentieth century, the Yangtze floods killed more than 500,000 people. The Three Gorges Dam reservoir, completed in 2006, limits the amount of water flowing out of it to try to lessen the risk of severe floods in areas downstream.

Vital statistics:

Three Gorges Dam

Cost: at least $25 billion
Length of dam: 7,660 feet (2,335 m)
Height of dam: 607 feet (185 m – as tall as a 60-story building)
Length of reservoir: 400 miles (660 km)
Reservoir capacity: 5 trillion gallons (18 trillion liters) of water

However, when heavy rains caused floods across the country in July 2010, killing 900 people and displacing nearly 10 million in other areas, the water rose so high that it was only 65 feet (20 m) below the dam's maximum capacity. So Chinese officials downgraded their claim that the dam would withstand the equivalent to the worst flood in China in 1,000 years, to the worst flood seen in 100 years.

Development fact

Using hydropower from the Three Gorges Dam instead of electricity generated by coal, China will avoid the emission of around 105 million tons (95 metric tons) of carbon dioxide a year – more than the annual output of Norway and Sweden put together.

Three Gorges hydropower

The Chinese government estimates that its power output needs to increase 8 percent every year in order to power its developing industries. China's main electricity source is coal-fired power plants, a major source of greenhouse gas emissions. The Three Gorges dam's hydroelectric power plant has the largest generating capacity in the world, producing about as much electricity as 22 large coal-fired plants. It can provide electricity for 10 percent of China's industries and about 150 million people.

River traffic

The dam raised the water level in the river for 1,400 miles (2,250 km) inland. Now large ocean-going, cargo-carrying ships can travel as far as the city of Chongqing, in central China. Around 90 percent of goods in and out of Chongqing are transported by water, because this is cheaper than other types of long-distance transportation. Chongqing has grown rapidly owing to river trade and expanding industries and also because hundreds of thousands of the people displaced by the dam moved there.

 This map shows the location of the Yangtze River and of the Three Gorges Dam.

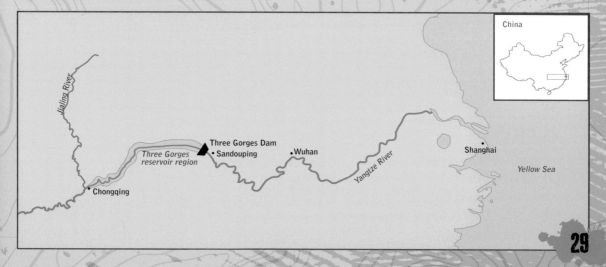

China

Jialing River

Three Gorges reservoir region

Three Gorges Dam
• Sandouping

• Wuhan

Yangtze River

• Shanghai

Yellow Sea

• Chongqing

Landslides

Two of the most significant problems associated with the Three Gorges Dam are landslides and earthquakes. As a reservoir is filled, water seeps into cracks in rocks and into soil, loosening slopes either side of the river until rocks and soil slide down. In the Yangtze region, the increasing number of landslides has been blamed on the dam. In 2003, a major landslide near the town of Qianjiangping on a tributary of the Yangtze capsized boats, destroyed factories, homes, and farmland, and killed 14 people.

Dozens more landslides occurred in 2006 after the water level was raised again, and in 2007, 31 people died when a landslide on a tributary in Hubei province crushed a bus. So far, experts have identified 9,000 areas where dangerous landslides could happen, and they say the risk of landslides could continue for 20 years, while land disturbed by the dam settles.

Local residents survey the scene of a landslide near the Three Gorges reservoir in China's Hubei province.

Earthquakes

Reservoirs can cause earthquakes. The weight of water in large reservoirs can increase pressure on existing faults deep in the Earth's crust. The pressure can vary with changes in the water level, causing further destabilization of faults. The Three Gorges Dam is built over the Jiuwanxi and the Zigui-Badong fault lines and, since the dam was built, there has been an increase in seismic activity in the region.

It is difficult to be certain of the exact cause of an earthquake, as seismic activity occurs so far below ground. However, since the dam was built, official monitoring stations have recorded many small-scale earthquakes, and deep cracks have appeared in roads and buildings by the river and its tributaries. So far, at least 50,000 people have been relocated because of seismic problems.

Destruction fact

The official figures suggest 1.3 million people were displaced by the dam's construction in 13 cities, 140 towns and 1,350 villages. The dam also submerged vast swathes of countryside and over a thousand rare architectural and archaeological sites.

Some geologists are also concerned that an earthquake might cause the Three Gorges Dam to collapse and cause a major flood that could kill millions of people. Dam engineers say that it was built to withstand an earthquake of 7.0 on the Richter scale. But small cracks keep appearing in the dam, and though most are repaired, they might undermine it.

The cracks in the wall of this farmer's home were caused by the building of the nearby Three Gorges Dam, which unsettled the delicate geology of the area.

Additional problems

The dam has created further issues. Because much of the river's silt now stays in the reservoir, coastal wetlands downstream are eroding. As the Yangtze delta collapses, seawater enters the river, affecting irrigation and drinking water. Because the dam slows the flow of the river, pollution from submerged areas, industries and homes concentrates in it, rather than washing out to sea.

Reservoir water is usually warmer in winter and cooler in summer than its river water. As reservoir water flows into its river, it alters river temperatures, creating conditions that are unnatural to local plants and animals. Pollution and changes in water flow and temperature threaten fish stocks. It may also contribute to the extinction of species such as the Yangtze River dolphin. There are even doubts about the dam's green credentials – decomposing submerged vegetation releases methane, a greenhouse gas that stores up to 25 times more heat in the atmosphere than the same volume of carbon dioxide.

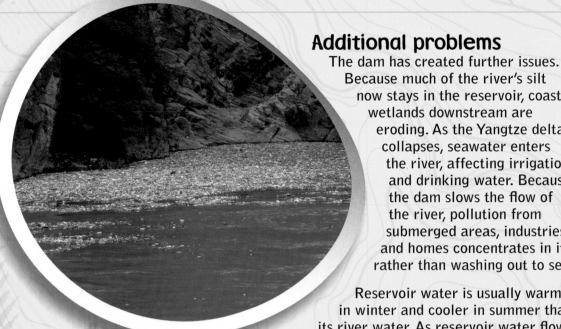

▲ The Three Gorges Dam exacerbates water pollution along the Yangtze River.

Alternatives

Critics of the Three Gorges Dam say there were alternatives. Some engineers argue that smaller and less problematic dams on the Yangtze tributaries could have generated as much power as the Three Gorges Dam and control flooding, too. Some even suggest that it would have been cheaper, cleaner and more productive for China to have invested in energy efficiency than in new hydropower plants.

ON THE SCENE

"We absolutely cannot relax our guard against ecological and environmental security problems sparked by the Three Gorges Project. We cannot win passing economic prosperity at the cost of the environment."

Wang Xiaofeng, Three Gorges Dam's head of construction, 2007

Lessons learned?

By 2011 the Chinese government had admitted that the Three Gorges Dam faced urgent geological, human and ecological problems that required the establishment of disaster warning systems, reinforcement of riverbanks and the displacement of more people. The dam was part of a larger scheme in China to build more than 100 large hydropower stations on the upper Yangtze basin. The question is whether problems with the Three Gorges dam have made the Chinese government wary of large-scale hydropower projects in the future.

EXPLORE FURTHER

Find out about the debate surrounding an earthquake that killed 80,000 people in Sichuan, China, in 2008. Was it triggered by nearby Zipingpu Dam?

Development or Destruction?

Development:

* The dam prevents some of the floods that killed over 500,000 people in the twentieth century.
* It can generate 10 percent of China's electricity.
* Using hydropower instead of coal saves 105 million tons (95 million metric tons) of CO2 a year.
* Expanding the river's transportation routes has developed trade and economy in the area.

Destruction:

* 1.3 million people have been displaced and historic sites submerged.
* Since the dam's construction, there have been an increased number of landslides and seismic events. Some fear an earthquake could cause the dam to collapse altogether.
* The dam causes problems such as coastal erosion and pollution.
* Cheaper, smaller damming schemes on Yangzae tributaries could have been as effective as the Three Gorges Dam.

Water redistribution, Spain

Spain uses huge quantities of water in the dry southern part of the country to irrigate economically important greenhouse crops, like tomatoes and lettuce. In order to meet this need in the future, the Spanish government has investigated various hydration possibilities. The Spanish National Hydrological Plan (SNHP) was to divert water from the rainy north of the country to the arid south.

△ Spain is one of the world's biggest producers and leading exporters of fruits and vegetables.

Dams and diversion

The Spanish government agreed on the SNHP in 2001. This entailed carrying water from the Ebro River in the northeast of the country, 500 miles (800 km) to the south. The plan involved building dams and hundreds of miles (kilometers) of canals and pipelines for over 20 water transfer projects.

Vital statistics:

SNHP

Cost: around $3.5 billion
Total number of projects: 889
Number of dams: 118
Number of canals: 14
Longest canal: 435 miles (700 km)
Longest pipeline: 560 miles (900 km)

Chapter 6

▽ In Spain, most tomato crops are grown in giant greenhouses covered with polythene.

The regions that would have benefited from the diversion include Murcia and Almería. Almería is hot and dry, with naturally barren soil and few rivers. Most of its water comes from underground aquifers. Almería is the closest thing in Europe to desert. The plan also included diverting water farther north to Spain's second largest city, Barcelona, which was short of water, too.

ON THE SCENE

"Water is to survive, to carry on. What we're asking for is not to get richer and richer, but to maintain what's been achieved. If we don't have water, we can't produce, and if we can't produce, we can't get any money and we have to emigrate."

Andrés Soler Márquez from vegetable growers Vega Cañada in Almería, 2004

Beneficiaries of the plan

The region of Almería is economically very important to Spain for growing water-hungry crops. Salad, for instance, is grown all year round in hundreds of square miles (square kilometers) of plastic greenhouses. The export value is around $3.3 billion per year. This is achieved with irrigation. The government subsidizes irrigation water for farmers in the region. It is 100 times cheaper than water for use in other industries, so farmers can produce cheap crops and make more profit.

The sunny climate also attracts tourists. Golf courses, hotels with swimming pools and other tourist developments along the coast are using far more water than local sources can provide. More recently, seawater has been getting into aquifers, and irrigation using this water is damaging crops. The supply of fresh water from the Ebro River is seen as essential for the future of the region.

Disappearance of the delta?

People living in and around the Ebro basin opposed the SNHP. One of the major concerns was that water diversion could speed up the drying out of the delta. Damming of the upper reaches of the Ebro River in the past had already reduced water flow by around 30 percent and trapped most of the sediment eroded from upriver.

This delta, like others, is formed when sediment is deposited on land at the place where rivers slow down and meet the sea. Without sediment deposition to maintain the delta, the delta is gradually lost. And with fewer nutrients washing into the sea with those sediments, there are fewer fish, such as sardines, in the Mediterranean near the mouth of the Ebro today than there were in the past.

The delta has economic importance because 60 percent of its area is used to intensively grow rice, a crop that requires damp soil. The Ebro Delta also has environmental importance. The Ebro Delta Natural Park wetland in Catalonia is the second largest national park in Spain and one of the most important wetlands in Europe. The delta has a variety of different ecosystems, including sand dunes, salt marshes and rice fields.

Over 80 percent of the Ebro Delta has been developed for agriculture and housing, and the rest consists of lagoons, reed beds, marshes and beaches.

More than 350 types of birds – around 60 percent of all bird species found in Europe – rest, feed or nest in or around the Ebro Delta.

Change of direction

In 2004, a new government was formed in Spain and it cancelled the Hydrological Plan. The political opposition was based partly on environmental and economic reasons, including the high cost of building the water transfer infrastructure. It was also because the plan went against a Europe-wide law against water transfers from one river basin to another. The government then announced a new water plan called AGUA, which stands for Actuaciones para la Gestión y la Utilización del Agua, meaning "Water Management and Use Actions." This plan could supply southern Spain with water without diversion of the Ebro River. In AGUA, half of the water would be supplied from 21 new desalination facilities, planned in provinces bordering the Mediterranean. These plants could turn seawater into fresh water.

Desalinated water in Spain

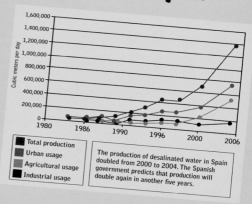

The production of desalinated water in Spain doubled from 2000 to 2004. The Spanish government predicts that production will double again in another five years.

Legend:
- Total production
- Urban usage
- Agricultural usage
- Industrial usage

This chart shows the steep rise in Spain's use of desalinated water. The Spanish government built the first desalination plant in Europe in the Canary Islands, to help encourage tourism development. By 2006, Spain was the fourth largest user of desalination technology in the world.

Innovations: Desalination

Desalination factories remove salt from seawater in different ways. Reverse osmosis plants use pumps to force seawater through a membrane (very fine filter) that traps the salt. Another method is distillation, in which seawater is boiled so that it evaporates into steam. When the steam condenses, it forms drops of fresh water.

◁ **A technician works in a desalination plant in Mallorca, Spain.**

Dams and Hydropower

Benefits of desalination

One of the main advantages of the AGUA plan over the SNHP was security of supply. Because of the abundant supply of seawater, desalination plants can guarantee a supply of fresh water, even in times of drought. Desalination plants can also supply fresh water of consistent quality, whereas water from reservoirs sometimes needs filtering. Desalination plants are quicker to build, especially in a country with considerable expertise in the desalination industry. They also avoid time-consuming disputes with environmentalists. The new political leaders claimed desalination would be a third of the price per cubic meter (cubic foot) of diverted water, although their opponents had claimed that diverted water would be a third of the price of desalinated water!

Disadvantages of the AGUA plan

The AGUA program will not require the flooding of towns and habitats, but it will cause environmental damage. Desalination machines and pumps to distribute water to fields use a lot of electricity, mainly provided by coal-fired power stations. It is estimated that the AGUA desalination infrastructure would increase Spain's CO_2 emissions by 5 percent. Also, desalination creates large amounts of concentrated salty brine, and this waste is usually dumped at sea. If this is not done carefully, living things that are sensitive to high salt concentrations, such as seagrass, can die.

A single acre (0.4 hectares) of seagrass can provide food and shelter to as many as 40,000 fish and 50 million small invertebrates! An increase in salinity can cause reduced leaf growth and disease in seagrass and other marine plants, and it can hamper their ability to make food by photosynthesis.

ON THE SCENE

"In 2005 there was a drought, and there was doubt that the Ebro River would even have had enough water to supply had the planned pipeline been built."

Claudio Klynhout, director of communications for AcuaMed, the department of the Spanish government in charge of the water program, 2005

Future for Spain's water

In southern Spain the demand for water is currently rising. This is in part because investors are creating large tourism developments in the region, including millions of new hotel rooms and new golf courses. The government plans to charge more for water used in tourism than for agriculture, yet it will put further stress on the region's supplies, even with the new desalination plants. The idea of Ebro transfer is still a possibility for easing water shortages. For example, following low rainfall in 2008, the government reconsidered, but did not go ahead with, diverting some Ebro water to Barcelona, which was part of the original SNHP.

▽ As the number of tourists to Spain increases, there will be even heavier demands on the country's limited water supply.

39

Sustainable futures

Storing water

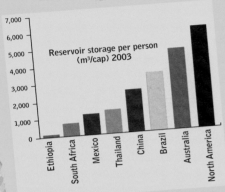

Reservoir storage per person
(m³/cap) 2003

(Bar chart showing values from 0 to 7,000 for: Ethiopia, South Africa, Mexico, Thailand, China, Brazil, Australia, North America)

Many LEDCs build reservoirs to develop their potential for water storage. Like Ethiopia, Australia has long periods without rain. But as we can see from the graph above, Australia has 100 times more water storage capacity per person. In Ethiopia, the lack of ability to store water has made the country vulnerable to dangerous droughts. This has been estimated to have caused a 38 percent decline in GDP and a 25 percent increase in poverty for 2003–2005 .

Water is one of the biggest sustainability issues the world faces for the future. As populations grow, water and energy demands will increase. Climate change may severely worsen the situation, with rising temperatures in some regions and changing rain patterns. Experts predict that irrigation demands will increase by between 50 and 100 percent by 2025 and the world will need almost 60 percent more energy in 2030 than in 2020. Do dams create too much destruction to be part of the solution?

Development fact

Dam building is a major reason that over a third of all freshwater fish are at risk of extinction.

World dams

The destructive impact of large dams became a major issue at the end of the twentieth century, and many more economically developed counties stopped building them. The story is different in less economically developed countries (LEDCs).

▽ Dam building is putting river wildlife, like this giant Mekong catfish, at risk.

Chapter 7

For example, almost 600 large dams were built within just two years (1999–2001) in Asia, where hydropower is needed now in order to develop as other regions did in the past.

Government initiatives

The obvious way to reduce the need for fresh water using dams and other methods is for governments, companies and individuals to reduce the amount of water they use. Governments can reduce water waste by lining canals to prevent leaks. They can also impose restrictions on water use. For example, in Nevada (pages 10–15), police issue fines to people who use hose pipes at times when watering is not allowed. In addition, they can encourage people to use less by introducing such measures as a sliding price scale, charging people more if they use more water.

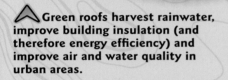

▲ Green roofs harvest rainwater, improve building insulation (and therefore energy efficiency) and improve air and water quality in urban areas.

Individual actions

There are many ways in which we can all save water. Fixing a dripping tap can reduce waste by up to 1,320 gallons (5,000 liters) of water a year. Taking a short shower rather than a bath, installing low-flush toilets, and only turning on dishwashers and washing machines when they are fully loaded all reduce water use as well. Turning off the tap while brushing your teeth or shaving can save up to 1.5 gallons (6 liters) of water per minute! Some households collect rainwater and use it for cleaning and watering plants or grow a green roof, which collects and stores water that can then be used for toilet flushing.

Destruction fact

Give up meat and save water! Just 500 gallons (2,000 liters) of water can grow food for a vegetarian for a whole day. It takes over 400 gallons (1,500 liters) to make just one quarter-pound burger!

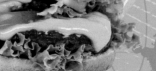

Dams and Hydropower

Industrial impacts

Farmers can reduce water use by improving irrigation, as many irrigation systems use double the amount of water crops really need. For example, drip irrigation systems carry drips of water directly to plant roots, and household wastewater can be used for irrigation after being cleaned in treatment plants. Farmers can also grow less thirsty crops, line and cover irrigation canals to reduce seepage, and water crops early or late in the day, when evaporation rates are less because it is cooler.

Alternatives and improvements

Critics of dams point to alternatives like the Chinese Dujiangyan irrigation system, built in 265 BCE. Barriers guide the Min River through artificial channels into numerous distributaries along the gently sloping plain. The system prevents floods, irrigates fields and only needs maintaining by dredging the river once a year to keep the water level constant. Supporters say dams can have less impact on the environment. For example, the Glomma and Laagan river basin dams in Norway enlarged existing lakes in uninhabited regions to make reservoirs, rather than submerging habitats.

ON THE SCENE

"We are in an era when we must produce more, and at the same time impact on the environment less."

Peter Kendall, president of the UK's National Farmer's Union, 2009

Innovations: Fish ladders

Dams such as Glomma and Laagen in Norway have fish ladders. A fish ladder is a series of low steps fish leap up to pass over dams so that important spawning-migration routes are not interrupted.

 Fish ladder, Norway.

Micro-hydropower plants

According to the US Geological Survey, in the future there may be more small-scale hydropower plants that generate electricity for single communities than large dams. For example, when the people of Bilgaon village in India got none of the power promised by the Narmada Valley dam project (pages 16–21), they built themselves a low-cost, small hydropower plant on a waterfall. It is low-impact and sustainable and is owned by the local community.

▲ The ancient Dujiangyan irrigation system is a **UNESCO** World Heritage Site.

Large dams in the future

Most people believe large dams still have an important role to play in providing drinking and irrigation water, flood control and power in the future. But how they achieve this will continue to be a subject of contentious debate. For example, China already has about half the world's large dams. To reduce its carbon output, it is planning new hydropower plants within China and building large dams in continents including Africa in return for resources such as oil and copper. Will these new projects cause similar environmental and social impacts as past projects? Will they include agreements between riparian countries about using and sharing dams and water, to avoid the disputes that some people predict for the future?

ON THE SCENE

"The issue of dams and their benefits and impacts has become one of the battlegrounds in the sustainable development arena."

Nelson Mandela, 2000

Debate club

Organize a debate to discuss the building of a new dam. You'll need six people to act as the characters below. They can use information from the book and the statements below to get started.

Each person should be given a chance to speak, without interruptions. Others in the class or group can listen to the speakers in the debate as if they are the developers. The developers have to decide at the end whose arguments are most convincing and if they will proceed with the dam project, and how.

TEENAGER

"Lots of people leave the village for jobs in the city. The dam will mean we can get local jobs in construction or hydropower, on fishing boats or in tourist businesses on the reservoir."

ENVIRONMENTALIST

"The reservoir will submerge a large area of forest and all the plants and animals living there."

OLDER WOMAN

"My family has lived here for 200 years, and I've got relatives buried in the valley. I don't want to leave my home and live in a lonely high-rise flat."

BIOLOGIST

"The dam will alter the temperature and quality of the water and threaten several rare breeds of fish in the river here"

FARMER

"With irrigation water for my fields, I'll be able to grow and sell more crops and improve my family's life.

BUSINESSWOMAN

"With hydropower from the dam, I can open a factory here. If it is successful, other businesses might move here and the development might benefit us all."

Glossary

aqueduct Bridge-like structure built for carrying water.

aquifer Underground layer of rock that is saturated with water and acts as a water source for a well or spring.

basin Area of land around a large river with streams and tributaries running into it.

climate change Changes in the world's weather patterns caused by human activity.

colony Country or area that is governed by another country.

condense To change from a gas to a liquid or solid.

delta Area of land where a river splits into smaller rivers before entering the sea.

desalination Process that converts salt water into fresh water.

displace To force people to move away from their home to another place.

drought Long period of time with no rain or very little rain.

ecosystem Community of living things and the environment in which they live, for example, a forest.

evaporation The change from a liquid into a gas; for example, water evaporates to form water vapor.

fault Long crack in the Earth's crust, or rocky surface.

GDP Abbreviation for Gross Domestic Product – the total value of goods and services produced by a country in one year.

generator Machine that produces electricity.

greenhouse gas Gas in the upper atmosphere that warms the lower atmosphere around Earth by trapping the sun's heat.

hydrologist Scientist who studies the Earth's water.

hydropower Electricity made using the energy of moving water.

irrigation Supplying water for crops and other plants.

irrigation system System of artificial pipes, ditches and channels to supply water to plants.

LEDC Less-economically developed country; a country where many people are poor and do not have access to services like schools and hospitals.

mega-dam Dam with a minimum height of 490 feet (150 meters).

Dams and Hydropower

nomad Someone who moves from place to place, instead of living in one fixed location.

precipitation Water falling to Earth in the form of rain, snow, hail or sleet.

renewable Something that can be replaced.

reservoir Lake built by people to store water.

riparian Living or located along the bank of a river.

runoff Water and dissolved fertilizers and other waste flowing into rivers and streams.

sanitation Disposal of sewage and other wastewater from people's homes.

sediment Tiny pieces of mud and rock that are carried by a river.

seismic Connected with or caused by earthquakes.

subsidize To give financial assistance to an industry with public money.

sustainable Using natural resources to meet the needs of the present without jeopardizing those resources for future generations.

thirsty crops Crops that need a lot of irrigation to grow.

tributary River or stream that flows into a larger river.

turbine Machine that uses water, wind or gas to turn a wheel or cylinder to create electricity.

United Nations (UN) International organization promoting peace, security and economic development.

water transfer Artificial conveyance of water from one area to another.

World Bank Organization that lends funds to provide help to poorer member countries.

Web sites

Due to the changing nature of Internet links, Rosen Publishing has developed an online list of Web sites related to the subject of this book. This site is updated regularly. Please use this link to access the list:

http://www.rosenlinks.com/dod/dams

Index

Dams and Hydropower